With best wishes,

John Paul Zahody
7-26-88

The Secret
of
Staying
Together

John Paul Zahody

The Secret
of
Staying
Together

John Paul Zahody

HeartLight Publications
Altadena, California

Illustrations by Nickie Hovhannessian

Typesetting by DynaType Telecom
Glendale, California

Printed in the U.S.A. by Kingsport Press
Kingsport, Tennessee

Library of Congress Catalog Card Number: 85-82014
ISBN: 0-9615911-0-2

10   9   8   7   6   5   4   3   2   1

Dedication

With Love and gratitude to
Doug Woolley, Helen Copeland,
Karen Wernicke, Lynn Skordal,
Keith Jones, Ginny Steele,
Ray Choiniere, and Christine Elizabeth,
who, in that order of appearance,
became my best friends in
this Lifejourney of Self-discovery
—all of you know in your hearts
how much you have contributed
to the substance of this book.

Contents

Introduction

You have opened this little book to find answers. Perhaps you are still young, single, and possessed of a clear and high ideal of the marriage relationship. Or you may be married and not very satisfied with the outcome of your time together with your mate. Or you might just now be trying to put your life together following a separation or divorce. Maybe you're someone who has already been through several of these, and now you find yourself somewhat disillusioned and cynical. Or you could be seriously considering going ahead with a second, third, fourth, or even fifth marriage, and saying to yourself, "Somehow it just *has* to work this time."

Whoever you are, you are likely to be

9

at least a little unsure of what it takes to have a happy and lasting marriage. So let me begin by saying that I respect you for taking interest in this book. It is my conviction that you would not be holding it in your hands at this moment if you weren't meant to benefit from its message. You will find that it has answers for you that you may have been seeking for most of your life.

Now this book is little for a very important reason. It has been created to be a constant companion to you, to be carried with you and deeply studied until *your own experience* confirms the truth of what is written in these pages.

I say this to you with the conviction borne of several years of demonstrating the truth of these principles in my own life, and seeing them proven again and again in the lives of those with whom I have worked as counselor and teacher.

Therefore I appeal to you, dear reader, to begin by setting aside at least one brief period of time each day to give your full attention to this message. Then, as your understanding increases, you will want to allow more time for study and contemplation of the principles presented here.

I am offering you the secret that will displace the doubt and fear in your heart. I am challenging you to discover the freedom and peace that have always been yours to claim. And I can promise that this will be your experience if you fulfill just one condition: you must be *ready* for it.

Are you ready?

You can find out quickly if you will just ponder this simple question and answer it for yourself: *Have the events of my life in this "School of Human Experience" so driven me to seek real understanding that I will not be denied?* If your answer to this question is an honest "yes," then you can be assured you are ready, and you will soon come to recognize that the principles which are the message of this little book have always been written in the depths of your own heart.

Discover them *there*, and you will be free of fear and open to the Way of Love in marriage, because you will have found *within yourself* the secret of staying together.

John Zahody
Altadena, California

Chapter One

The Secret

There is one principle, one fact of life, which *is* the secret of staying together, and you will not have to search beyond this page to find it. I present it to you here as the starting point for everything that will be said in the chapters that follow:

Mutual commitment is the identity of every lasting relationship.

Now this statement probably seems simple enough to you. In fact, you may already be thinking you understand it pretty well, but I ask you not to draw any final conclusions until you have finished reading this book and then listened closely to the testimony of your own heart.

For now, I would like you to take a few moments to consider the word "identity" as I have used it in the statement above. Perhaps you'll find that you're in some doubt about how a relationship can have *its own identity* apart from those of the two individuals involved. And here we have the essence of what makes this principle a secret—the fact that *a relationship has its own identity which is the mutual commitment of its partners* seems to be unknown to most people.

Therefore, need we wonder why so many so-called marriages fail, since almost nobody knows what a marriage really *is!* Now, of course, there are millions of people who say that "commitment" is the basic requirement for a successful relationship, but after almost a decade of careful observation and study, I am convinced beyond all doubt that very few of us have ever learned what that word means. Yet my dictionary offers a very clear and concise definition. It says that to "commit" means "to pledge; to bind; as to commit oneself to a certain course."

"To bind"? Hmmm.

In our freedom-conscious society, not many people like the idea of being bound by anything or anyone. But notice where this binding takes place—the dictionary example reveals that we commit *ourselves.* Therefore, commitment is something that takes place *within yourself,* so it can only be *to* yourself, *for* yourself, and never outside of yourself to someone else. It depends on no one but you. Again, *you do not commit to anyone but yourself.*

So it follows that, in a true relationship of marriage, *mutual commitment is two individuals each independently pledging or binding themselves "to a certain course,"* as the dictionary puts it, that course being an agreement to be faithful partners in the joining of their lives, both socially and physically, which agreement is commonly called a contract or covenant of marriage.

Now it is important that you have a good understanding of what you have just read before going on, so please take time to read it again if any part of it is unclear to you. Remember, you have invested your time and your money in this book for the specific purpose of replacing your doubt about relationships with the certainty of direct *knowing* by your own experience, so this is no occasion to be haphazard in your approach to this study. There isn't any good reason to hurry; you are just now beginning to call forth from deep within yourself the strong foundation of principle that will become your bedrock of security and peace of mind in every type of relationship you will ever have. So I encourage you to take your time and do it right.

In the light of the definitions given, let

us now consider what a marriage is *not:* it is not living together and having children; it is not the sexual union of a man and a woman; it is not the ceremony that makes it all "official"; it is not the words spoken during the ceremony—neither the vows taken nor the pronouncements of the person officiating; it is not the license issued by the state; it isn't even all of these things taken together.

Any normal man and woman could set up housekeeping for a couple of years, have sexual relations, and produce children, couldn't they? And what is this by itself? Nothing more than a social arrangement and basic biology. As precious as the lives of the children are, and as pleasurable as the social arrangement and the sexual relationship might be, somehow we still don't have a marriage here, do we? And what about the ceremony? By itself, it is nothing more than a sequence of words and procedures. A group of competent actors could get through it quite convincingly, and probably very few of us would be able to tell the difference. And the license? By itself, a blood test and some paperwork, that's all.

Nowhere in any of these things can we *identify* a marriage. No matter how important we may consider any or all of them to be, the *identity* of the marriage just isn't there, is it? Instead, it is to be found in the genuine mutual commitment established between its two partners.

At this point you might be moved to ask some very pointed questions, like, "Where does this genuine mutual commitment come from? How is it established and maintained?"

"How can I determine whether or not the declarations of commitment made by my partner and myself are the real thing?"

"Am I even capable of being part of such a relationship?"

"Why am I so afraid of committing myself? Is there anything I can do about this fear?"

The remaining chapters of this book are devoted to answering these questions.

Chapter Two

The
Foundation
Stone

Mutual commitment, the identity of every lasting relationship, rests upon a foundation stone. And, surprisingly enough, it is the same foundation stone that supports the existence of the universe and everything in it.

That foundation stone is *Integrity.*

The whole universe has Integrity—its components are "integrated," or *"united* so as to form *a complete or perfect whole,"* as my dictionary says. In other words, they co-exist within a *system of order.* So we are able to recognize that *order is always the primary evidence of Integrity.*

From the immensity of galaxies all the way down to the tiniest atom, there is order established. Indeed, the purpose of every truly scientific investigation ever undertaken by humankind has been to discover and learn to understand the system of order behind some condition or phenomenon. This order is assumed to exist, otherwise what good would the discovery be? Without order, the information gained could not be understood or intelligently applied—it would have no meaning or usefulness.

Sooner or later, each of us makes the simple yet startling discovery that, being a system of order, *the universe is designed to work, therefore all systems within it are designed to work.*

The true relationship of marriage is a phenomenon of human life. It is a *system of order.* It is therefore *designed to work!* Otherwise there could be no such thing as a successful marriage. Now, since order always comes from Integrity, the *commit-*

ment of the partners which establishes and identifies this system of order must therefore come from the *Integrity* of the partners. So we can say that *commitment is an expression of Integrity.*

The Integrity of your mind and heart

Most of us have observed Integrity and commitment operating in human affairs in the form of honesty, fairness, consistency, and excellence of performance. And why do we value these traits of character so highly? Because we have recognized that they bring order, harmony, and fulfillment into our lives.

Ultimately, we come to understand that the conditions of order and harmony we experience individually are nothing other than accurate *reflections* of the Integrity we have individually *realized* and *practiced.* Just as the mirror in your bedroom faithfully reflects your outer (physical) character, so do the affairs of your life faithfully reflect your inner (mental/emotional) character. Like everything else, this reflection phenomenon happens because of the *system of order* which underlies it. Now, if you are ready to look closely at your own experience with an open mind and heart, you are going to see this fact demonstrated over and over in the events of your life. Indeed, it will one day become completely obvious to you if it is not already.

Long ago, a wise teacher described this system of order with these words: *"With what measure you measure, it will be measured to you."* Now, if this is an accurate statement of principle, I can reverse the order and apply it to myself by saying, *"What is being measured to me must be what I have been measuring."*

Does this mean that if someone steals

from me, I must also be a thief? Of course not. But it may very well mean that within myself I am "measuring" a fear of loss, and it is this belief, this inner image of fear, that is being mirrored in the outer event of the theft. Again, you are going to have to study your own past and present experience in order to discover this truth for yourself.

Now I am going to say something to you that will prove to be one of the most important statements you will read in this book. The statement is this: *You cannot not have Integrity.*

Regardless of your past experience or how you see yourself now, I will tell you again, YOU CANNOT NOT HAVE INTEGRITY. Think about it for a moment. Life is an orderly phenomenon, is it not? Therefore, Life has Integrity. And you are Life in the form of an individual. Look at the functions of your body. You have a respiratory *system*, a circulatory *system*, a glandular *system*, voluntary and involuntary nervous *systems*, etc., all of them manifestations of *order*— all of them magnificent expressions of the *Integrity of Life*. Now does it make sense to believe that there is no system of order (Integrity) for your mind and heart, which make up your *consciousness*—your *awareness*—the highest activity of your whole existence?

It makes no sense at all!

On the contrary, the Integrity of your mind and heart stands clearly revealed as the character of all of your genuine ideals. It can also be seen in the working of the "measuring" principle just described: *"With what measure you measure, it will be measured to you."* Your beliefs, feelings, judgments, and consequent actions determine your individual conditions of life, and this system of order cannot be violated, any more than you can cancel the law of gravity. This is your Integrity in action, constantly surrounding you with a mirror image of your inner self. So no matter how often you and I may have failed to live up to our ideals, our Integrity remains forever intact. This is why we experience conflict within ourselves when we act in ways that do not express the harmony and order of Integrity. Because of the Integrity of Life— which is your life and mine—any form of dishonesty, unfairness, inconsistency, or mediocrity we may be practicing keeps us from being at peace with ourselves—our sense of well-being is disturbed—and this *dis*-order is bound to be *reflected* in our physical bodies and in the circumstances of our daily lives. On such occasions, we begin to feel confused, which is to say, *separated* from order, instead of feeling *integrated* with the order and harmony of Life Itself.

It is this "integrated" feeling, this sense of wholeness, this peace of mind and heart that every one of us is seeking, whether we realize it or not.

Why?

Because it already exists within us as the very character of our Life, consequently we long to bring it forth into expression. Just as the image of an ideal fires the imagination of the artist and inspires him or her to give it tangible form, so does the Integrity of Life continually press upon us from within to let *It* be the character of all that we feel and think, in order that It may be *expressed* in the form of what we say and do, and *reflected* in outer conditions of order, peace, and harmony. However, like the artist, *we must first become aware of the image of our ideal before we can express it in the activity of our lives.* And here we come to the very core of the

purpose of this book, which is to clarify
the image of the marriage ideal for all who
are ready to dis-cover (uncover) it within
themselves and let it come forth in the form
of lasting relationships that *work*—marriages
that can be *identified* by the *mutual
commitment* of their partners.

Can you "try" marriage?

Nowadays there are those who say that
marriage is just a carryover from antiquity,
and therefore no longer relevant in our so-
called "Age of Enlightenment." Usually the
current divorce statistics are offered as hard
evidence of its being outdated, and often-
times we hear "reasoning" which reduces
to something like, "I *tried* it, so *I know*
it doesn't work." Or perhaps the more
fashionable variation, ". . . it doesn't work
for me." (To "try" marriage means, of
course, that you start off saying to yourself

[sometimes unconsciously], "Well, I can always get a divorce if it doesn't work.")

Now if this comes close to being your current position, I would simply like to ask, how do you know for sure that the "it" you (and all those statistical "other people") *tried* was really *marriage* in the first place? Have you considered the possibility that our society's miserable track record in marriage might be due to our almost complete ignorance of what it *is?*

Let's really open our minds right now and look at the whole picture. People by the millions pair off each year to "try" something they call *marriage*, which, in its true state, *is identified by the mutual commitment of its partners.* Now would you like to tell me just how one "tries" a commitment? This is an illogical absurdity, isn't it? Utterly ridiculous! We plainly cannot have "try" and a real marriage at the same time, can we?

Therefore, who among all these people who have "tried and failed" was really married?

NOT ONE OF THEM!

Look, why don't we just admit it once and for all: what we have are millions of unknowing people being pronounced "man and wife," who should instead be declared "hopeful roommates." Oh yes, they may speak about their mutual devotion until they drop from exhaustion. But when they get all through, they *still* won't have a marriage, will they?

Why?

Because a real marriage doesn't exist until there is mutual commitment. Now, as you recall from the previous chapter, to *commit* means "to pledge; to bind; as to commit oneself to a *certain* course." See if you can find a trace of "try" in that anywhere!

Let's really be honest with ourselves here, shall we? How many storybook beginnings have we seen end in disaster? Excruciating emotional upheavals, unprecedented family violence, and a snowballing population of confused children growing up deeply afraid because of the almost total absence of anything like stability in their lives! Now I ask *you*, when are we, as a society, going to wake up and admit we know practically nothing at all about marriage?

When we've suffered enough from our ignorance to be willing to give it up . . . when the few among us who have understood and successfully *lived* the marriage principle really begin to be *seen* by the rest . . . when books like this one are thoughtfully studied by thousands more people like you, *that's when.* And until then, let's stop pretending that uncommitted relationships are marriages when we know in our hearts they are not!

You *can* be sure

Of course, today it is commonly believed that no one entering a marriage can ever really be sure it will last, no matter how sincere both partners may be in their vows of commitment. Indeed, many people think it would be foolishly impractical for them to commit themselves to the kind of relationship we have identified here as marriage, especially in these "uncertain times."

But are you beginning to see why the times are so *uncertain?* The state of the times begins and ends with the state of the individual, doesn't it? Therefore, we as individuals must first be *certain* of the meaning and value of marital commitment. *Then* our Integrity can bring the *certainty*

of order to our marriages, and thereby, to
the times.

Remember our discussion of the
"measuring" principle earlier in this chapter?
"With what measure of Integrity we measure
to others, *in that measure* will Integrity be
measured to us." Yes, for all the seeming
disorder and uncertainty, the universe
remains an orderly place. Integrity *is*. It is
certain and It is constant. So I say to you
that *any lack of order, commitment, or
Integrity on the part of others that has
disturbed the order of your life is a precise
reflection of the beliefs and/or practices
which you have been "measuring" in your
daily affairs.*

Contrary to popular "folk wisdom," the
"measuring" principle reveals the real truth
to be *believing is seeing,* and not the other
way around. That is, *what we believe and
expect becomes our experience.* And as

many of us have already discovered, the more we practice *living* according to our highest sense of Integrity, the more Integrity we experience from others.

"Does this mean I determine what every person does in his or her relationship with me?"

No, it means *you determine the quality of your own experience.* Please note that the statement above reads, *"any lack . . . that has disturbed the order of your life. . . ."* To state it in positive terms, the more you believe in—and practice living from—your own Integrity, the more you will come to believe in—and experience—the Integrity of others. And *the less disturbed the order of your life will be* on those occasions when someone seems to fall short of the mark with you. Because of the *order* measured and established by *your* practice of Integrity, these occurrences will simply have no power to measure *dis*order into your experience. On the contrary, they will appear to resolve themselves to your greatest advantage, and people who do not understand the principle will begin to call you "lucky."

Is Integrity the *theme* of your daily life? (Notice that I did *not* ask you if you were performing perfectly in all areas. I asked about the *theme* of your life—the dominant character, attitude, flavor of what you think and feel and say and do.) Is yours the way of honesty, fairness, consistency, and excellence, or isn't it? Do you keep your agreements? Is your word good? How consistent are you? Is it your standard practice to give your best to the work you do? To your family and friends? To those you have undertaken to serve in business and in your personal life? What do you *believe* about your Integrity? About the Integrity of others you know, especially those of the opposite sex? What basic expectations do you have in your relationships with others? Stop right here and take time to ponder these questions carefully before continuing. . . .

Are you beginning to see how your relationships came to be what they were and are? Can you now acknowledge that, in order to have commitment in a relationship, you must first have it in the way you live your individual life? It is a fact that *your ability to recognize the Integrity of true commitment in yourself and in your partner comes directly from your own daily practice of Integrity—from the quality of commitment to honesty, fairness, consistency, and excellence of performance that prevails in your personal affairs. This* is how you can eliminate your fear and uncertainty about marriage. *This* is how you can be sure!

Indeed, how else? How could you possibly hope to identify something with which you are not personally familiar?

Obviously, the more you practice anything, the better you know that which you are practicing. And the better you know it, the more secure you will be in knowing you can recognize it in yourself and others. Through practice, you will also become increasingly sensitive to the guiding inner signals of Intuition which come from your Integrity. Accordingly, you will experience a deep sense of Peace (inner order) when you are acting according to the ordered wisdom of Integrity. And you will seem to lose your Peace whenever you embark upon a course of action which is out of harmony with this wisdom. Of course, you must learn to distinguish this true sense of Peace from common feelings of human comfort before you can rely upon this wonderful way of guidance.

As you have no doubt realized by now, marriage is definitely not child's play. It is for mature adults only. There is little room for the pride, arrogance, and personal judgment so typical of those who are still not in close touch with their Integrity. Marriage requires a good measure of humility, as does the honest self-observation I have advocated in this chapter.

Awareness is power

"So what can I do about the things I find in myself that need correcting? I've been this way most of my life, you know, and nothing I've tried has ever made much difference."

The answer to this dilemma is contained in the above adaptation of the classic saying, "Knowledge is power."

I'm sure you recall that there are many things you did as a child, which you no longer do. You say instead, "Now I know better." So just what is this "Now I know better" experience? It is nothing other than *clear awareness of yourself—and what you are doing—in the light of Principle. And this is the power of Integrity which corrects disorder in your life.* How do you get it? By honest, persistent, compassionate self-observation, questioning yourself as I have suggested, until Integrity again brings you to "Now I know better." If you're ready, it is that simple. But if you're not, don't worry. You *will* be ready when you get sufficiently fed up with your suffering. So ask yourself, "What am I going to do about it *right now?*" And don't move until you get an answer.

Integrity is truly the foundation stone of Life. It provides for order in every facet of our human experience. In the marriage relationship, Integrity is expressed through the mutual commitment of a man and a woman, who individually pledge themselves to be faithful to the social and physical joining of their lives in an exclusive lifelong relationship.

Is it an ideal of yours to have a beautiful marriage? Is this something your heart deeply desires to see fulfilled, independent of social and cultural conditioning? If so, then I challenge you to study this chapter until its message is clear to you. Contemplate what it means to *"know thyself,"* as the oracle of ancient Greece advises. These two words are a concise summary of what you have just read. Understand their wisdom and you hold the key to success, not only in marriage, but in all the affairs of your life.

Chapter Three

Trust

The mutual commitment which *identifies* a relationship as a marriage rests upon the foundation stone of Integrity, the character of Life possessed (though not always expressed) by every one of us.

Now what about the all-important issue of *trust?* Again, my dictionary puts us right on the mark, because it defines trust as "assured reliance on another's *integrity.*" In marriage, of course, this factor of trust also carries the dimension of permanence. So, obviously, it would not be wise for you to marry until you determine that you and your prospective partner are *committed* to maintaining this relationship of trust throughout life. And this you can do only if you are living from your own highest sense of Integrity, as explained in the previous chapter. To paraphrase the definition of *trust*, your "assured reliance" on one another's Integrity with respect to your marriage contract can only exist on the basis of your *mutual commitment* to that contract, since *this commitment is what expresses your Integrity.*

Intention versus commitment

Now let's look at what typically happens when a couple calls their uncommitted arrangement a "marriage" and tries to make it work. First of all, they might say with great fervor that they are committed, but upon questioning them we discover that what they are really talking about is *intention. Sincere* intention, *persistent* intention, *fervent* intention, perhaps, but still just the *intention* to stay together and make it work.

You see, what they have called "commitment" has some "ifs" in it, all of which are variations of "*If* it doesn't work, we can always get a divorce." In other words, they *intend* to *try* to have a successful marriage. So once again we're back to the impossibility of "trying" a commitment. And the usual argument is, "Well, we have to be *realistic* nowadays, don't we?"

But where does this being "realistic" leave them? It leaves them in a perpetual state of doubt, which is temporarily concealed by the optimistic zeal of their mutual *intention,* mislabeled "commitment." On this basis they *try* to trust one another, but since intention alone can never offer any grounds for "assured reliance on another's integrity," the hidden doubt begins to surface as they experience the inevitable conflicts that arise in any relationship. So each of these once-hopeful partners is left to wonder if the other can really be trusted. . . .

"Will he respect my individuality when I disagree with him?"

"Will she always be faithful to me even though her work brings her into contact with men who are more successful than I am?"

"When we get older, will he tire of me and want someone younger and more attractive than I?"

"Does she really appreciate me after all the things I've done for her, or does she just take them for granted?"

So it is that the original attempt to trust gives way to the presence of doubt, which quickly becomes translated into some form of *fear of loss*—loss of acceptance, loss of respect, loss of freedom, loss of "this relationship in which I have invested so much of my life."

The legacy of ignorance

Without a solid foundation for trust, this feeling of fear can only increase. The partners' priority within the relationship shifts from *exploring and learning about themselves and one another* in this adventure called Life to *protecting and defending themselves* against impending loss. Thus the so-called marriage moves ever more rapidly toward a painful crisis, and the suffering of the partners becomes the suffering of their children, close relatives, and friends.

It is an ugly business, this widespread misunderstanding about marriage. In recent years, our young people have collectively been described as "The 'Me' Generation," largely because of a prevailing self-protective attitude spawned by the marital wasteland of our present society.

But what else could you expect?

Ask yourself, how often have they been able to see the outcome of lives committed to the practice of Integrity? Where were they to find honesty, fairness, consistency, and excellence to be the rule instead of the exception? Just how many living examples have they seen to inspire them to discover their own inner Integrity and the joyous fulfillment of living from It?

Because of our own ignorance, we have brought them forth into a vast desert of false values, where wealth and fame are glorified as idols to be sought after and worshipped. Where the outrageous behavior of their entertainers is the only expression of supposedly creative individuality that many of them can find to admire. Where "You can't trust anyone over 30" became their byword. Where the ignorant abandonment of the sanctity of marriage has brought about growing epidemics of new, sexually transmitted diseases such as herpes and

AIDS. Where lack of understanding has led to increased betrayal of trust and resentment between the sexes, and these conditions have been passed on by example to so many of our children. Is it really *that* hard for you to understand why more and more multiplied thousands of them feel their sexual energy so strongly directed toward members of their own sex? And the tragic irony of it all is that the older "straight" population's penchant for misunderstanding, resentment, and condemnation of homosexuals and lesbians is nothing more than a redirection of the same ignorant attitudes that brought them into being in the first place!

The answer is simple

Now it is time to give first priority to finding out how we can begin to reverse these deplorable conditions. It is time to demand Integrity from ourselves as individuals. It is time for us to admit that we have so very much to learn about marriage and family life. Which means we're going to have to give up a great quantity of "what we 'know' that just ain't so," to paraphrase Will Rogers.

It is time for us to discover that, contrary to most "educated" opinion, the answer is simple.

"My people are *destroyed* for lack of knowledge," declares the voice of Deity in ancient Scripture. Isn't that simple enough? Notice that it does not say we are destroyed for lack of sincerity or good intention or trying. It says "lack of *knowledge*"! It says *destruction comes from ignorance.* That's all. Nothing mysterious or complicated about it.

Now remember, we have already observed that self-awareness, *self-knowledge* (which means to *"know* thyself" in the light of Principle) *is the power of Integrity within us which corrects destructive disorder in our lives.* And obviously, this process of correction must begin with you and me in our marriages, families, and personal affairs, otherwise we have no hope of seeing our society corrected.

Fundamentally, we have been talking about the restoration of *trust* in human relationships, with special emphasis on marriage. Now it is up to you, through your own experience, to discover that you must first come to know and trust your own Integrity before you can know the lifelong mutual trust of a genuine marriage. *Through consistent self-observation and practice, your Integrity must become the character of your daily life.*

Begin to *"know* thyself" in this way, and before many days have passed, you will experience a deep inner *Peace*, which will grow to become *the very compass of your life.* Then you will know how, when, and with whom to commit yourself in the true relationship of marriage. You will recognize Integrity to be the character of your partner's life because you have first come to *know* It as the character of your own. With such a foundation as this, both of you will *know* the permanence of your mutual commitment, and the trust established by it will likewise endure through all the days of your married life.

Chapter Four

Unconditional
Acceptance

The excitement of new romance. Court-ship. Mutual commitment. The marriage ceremony. Then comes what I have called "the challenge of becoming good room-mates." Even if the partners were living together before their marriage, they must now adapt to the new atmosphere of being *committed-for-life* roommates, which they will discover to be very much like starting over.

Becoming good roommates means observing one another's behavior patterns daily at very close range, feeling appreciation when we *like* what we see and disappoint-ment when we don't, and *learning to ex-perience all of these things without holding judgments of right or wrong.* This is the very essence of the *art* of friendship (and therefore, of marriage), and it is called *unconditional acceptance.*

"I'm right—you're wrong!"

Practicing unconditional acceptance in marriage becomes a major challenge for most of us, because, from early childhood, we have learned by example to make value judgments about ourselves and others. And this we do in order to gain some idea of how well (or how poorly) we're doing in life. We are conditioned to seek a sense of self-worth based on judgmental comparison of ourselves with others, and we try to maintain it by winning the approval of those whose judgments are important to us. As a result, we often feel vulnerable and insecure about ourselves, since our sense of well-being depends so much upon others giving us this approval. We also judge others to protect ourselves from being injured by their criticism and *dis*approval. Our tendency to judge thus becomes one of our first lines of defense, and we soon discover this to be a predominant theme throughout our society.

So it is that after years of practicing this self-protective judgment, a man and woman find themselves together as partners in a marital relationship, observing one another with greater concern, perhaps, than they have ever felt before in their adult lives. And why is that? Because they have said "I will, for keeps" to each other. Which makes them *vitally* interested in finding out as much as they can about what—and whom—they have gotten themselves into.

But, alas, the old habit of judging this "good" and that "bad" comes increasingly into the picture, and begins to fill up the space within each of them that should be occupied by a growing, *non-judgmental* understanding of one another. It becomes almost a knee-jerk reaction for both husband and wife to think "you're wrong" in response to behavior they don't like, instead of dropping all judgment in favor of trying to understand the reasons for that behavior. Of course, the "judge" often believes he (she) already understands the other's "problem" extremely well, and does not hesitate to say so. Thus "home" becomes the primary battleground of their lives instead of being the haven of rest they so deeply desire it to be. "I'm right—you're wrong" defines the position of both partners, and at first, each of them may be very surprised that the other refuses to "see the light," accept defeat, and surrender his (her) position.

Yes, it's a power struggle, pure and simple. And the war continues until its futility becomes apparent, and *the inher-*

ent strength of the marriage commitment brings husband and wife together to find a solution. That is, since neither of them is going to leave, they have this very fact as a strong, secure basis from which to work. So they decide they might as well get busy and do something about their problem, rather than continue indefinitely to put up with it.

With this kind of trust in the Integrity of their mutual commitment, they find that they are able to face the formidable challenge of reversing that age-old pattern of belief and behavior which has been among their primary means of self-protection. They can begin to move from *judging* right and wrong to *learning* more about one another's experience. To do this, of course, both partners must become actively interested in making this transition—they must sincerely want to understand rather than to judge. And this is *exactly* what it costs to enjoy harmony, intimacy, and fulfillment in marriage.

I wonder if you are now beginning to understand more deeply *the secret of staying together?* Can you see how essential mutual commitment is to "sticking with it" until judging gives way to unconditional acceptance? Think about it! Why would you bother to invest that kind of effort and energy in a relationship that might be over by next year? Can you see why almost nobody else does?

What unconditional acceptance is

Unconditional acceptance is abdicating your "judgeship" of right and wrong, because you finally realize it just doesn't work. It brings you nothing you really want and a great deal that you *don't* want. It has never helped anybody, reformed anybody, or won anybody's confidence in a relationship. But it *has* alienated *everybody!*

Unconditional acceptance is being willing to give your attention to your partner— to listen intently and ask questions because you want to understand his (her) experience, not gather evidence to cement your case against him (her).

Unconditional acceptance starts with dropping the judgments you have against yourself, because you want to understand the reasons behind what YOU do and don't do. And doesn't it make sense that if you first have this kind of respect for yourself, you will find it more and more natural to extend the same to your mate? So once again we are back to "know thyself."

Unconditional acceptance is remembering that neither you, your partner, nor anyone else can ever be without Integrity, and it is upon this Integrity that all your trust is founded. This is the spirit of true friendship. It is learning to allow *everyone* in your life to discover more and more of his own Integrity without the pressure of personal judgment coming from you.

Unconditional acceptance comes into your marriage relationship through much practice and patience and, yes, much forgiveness. Like your experience of Integrity, mutual commitment, and trust, it begins with your compassionate acceptance, observation, and understanding of yourself.

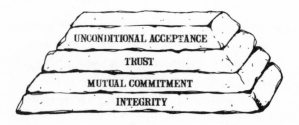

UNCONDITIONAL ACCEPTANCE

TRUST

MUTUAL COMMITMENT

INTEGRITY

Chapter Five

Acknowledgment

Now let's assume for the moment you're already married, and consider some typical complaints you might have. For instance, does his work seem to be more important to him than you are?

Does she sometimes not listen to you when you're saying something "important" to her?

Does he often appear to be insensitive to you and inconsiderate of your feelings?

Is she seemingly unable to look at a problem logically and objectively, without getting emotional?

Does he seldom acknowledge your efforts to look especially attractive?

Does she frequently seem displeased with what you have to say and how you say it?

Is he *ever* going to stop leaving his dirty socks on the floor? . . .

So there you are. Your mate seems to be raining on your parade. And you are facing a choice. You can "follow the herd," judging him (her) to be "wrong" and hating "the nasty problems he (she) causes." Or you can begin to regard such conflicts as valuable opportunities to practice unconditional acceptance and thus enrich the friendship of your marriage. These are your basic choices—now what are you going to do this time?

Golden wisdom

Well, why not start by asking yourself what you would want from your partner if the situation were reversed? Then just do that. In most cultures of the world, this simple wisdom holds a place of high honor. In ours it is called the "Golden Rule."

Have you ever really understood why?

Is it *golden* just because it requires you to be good to others? Or could it be the Golden Key to having the kind of life your heart truly desires? In modern language it reads, *"Always treat others as you would like them to treat you."* Could this be the highest form of *"With what measure you measure, it will be measured to you"?* What would you have done differently in your life if you had grown up knowing *this* about the Golden Rule, instead of regarding it merely as a way of allowing people to take unfair advantage of you?

The way to have your heart's desire "measured to you" is simply to let what you desire be the standard for "what you measure"! In marriage, it is the Integrity of your mutual commitment that establishes this "measuring" of your ideal between you and your partner. And if you practice this principle with everyone else in your life, you will find that those who are not yet ready to respond "in like measure" will automatically begin to drop out of your life so as to give place to others who are.

The value of acknowledgment

Now, with this deeper understanding, let's return to those marital "problems" we were considering at the start of this chapter. Of course, when conflict appears, what you want most from your partner is *acknowledgment.* That is, you want him (her) to honor you and your point of view as having value, whether he (she) agrees with you or not. And this is nothing less than *unconditional acceptance in action.* Genuine acknowledgment denies place to judgment and rejection, and gives expression to trust. In the light of the Golden Rule as we now understand it, you can plainly see that you must choose to start accepting your partner as he (she) is; you must acknowledge him (her); and you must do these things just as you would have them done for you—without looking back to keep score on who's doing what for whom! The Golden Rule applied in this way—"Always acknowledge others as you would like them to acknowledge you"—works to your greatest advantage, since "with what measure of acknowledgment you measure, the same will be measured to you." This you can begin to test and prove for yourself right now in the laboratory of your own daily life.

Because of the strong tendency toward judgment that prevails in our society, this principle directly challenges long-established patterns of belief and thought. Therefore, it may seem to be much easier to avoid than to face this challenge, since, at first, even positive change can be quite uncomfortable. Which is why so many people "drag their feet" until a crisis arises or their own suffering becomes unbearable. *Then* their awakening begins.

But it need not be so with you. Remember that *awareness is power.* What you have read thus far is more than sufficient for you discover within yourself the priceless value of choosing to accept others uncondition- ally instead of judging them. Without this acceptance, acknowledgment has no foun- dation from which to operate in marriage. But with it, acknowledgment comes as naturally as "wet" comes with water. And marital fulfillment is what happens when husband and wife learn to express their un- conditional acceptance of one another in the form of consistent acknowledgment.

Acknowledgment says, "I recognize your experience as having value because I accept unconditionally your value as an individual. I do not judge you. Though I may sometimes disagree with what you say and do, I continue to respect you. I know you cannot be without Integrity because Life cannot be without It. Therefore, regardless of our differences, I will always believe in you."

Chapter Six

Productive
Communication

For many years there have been hundreds of worthwhile classes, courses, seminars, and workshops providing married couples with instruction in the principles and techniques of effective communication. These programs have been attended by hundreds of thousands of hopeful people, who listened very intently as they were taught how productive communication works, what it looks and sounds like, and how to do it. Then most of them went home, put their notebooks on the shelf, and took up the same dreary lives they were living before, as if nothing had happened!

Why?

Because with all the valuable information they received, the one thing they needed most was still missing, and not even the world's greatest seminars and teachers could have given it to them. You know, of course, that what they still lacked was *the motivation to change!* These couples simply did not have enough desire to put the new information into practice. Which is not so difficult to understand when you realize that, in most cases, their relationships were not based upon genuine mutual commitment. Therefore, they were without a solid foundation for trust, unconditional acceptance, and acknowledgment. Now picture yourself in this position and let me ask you again: why would you bother to invest any considerable effort and energy in a relationship that might be over by next year? After all, you feel vulnerable enough as it is, don't you? So why on earth would you take a chance on "sticking your neck out" that far?

Certainly, learning all you can about the

process of productive communication can be a valuable step toward marital harmony, but *only if you've got a good enough reason to do what it takes to make it work!* Of course, if your relationship is truly "for keeps," you and your partner already have an excellent incentive to invest the necessary effort and energy, since the return on your investment will continue to grow throughout your life. Just keep this in mind, and you'll *have* the motivation to change your nonproductive communication patterns as you become aware of your capabilities and the many wonderful benefits that await you.

The power of acknowledgment

As we look into the process of productive communication, one of the first things we discover is that it begins with *acknowledgment* of the kind just described in the previous chapter. For instance, when someone with whom you disagree sincerely acknowledges you and your point of view as having value, you are immediately more receptive to that person, aren't you? In that moment there are no judgments for you to resist, therefore, you find yourself more open to the inner voice of your own Integrity, which is always moving you to give acknowledgment. So you respond in kind. Now your communication has become highly productive with just this one exchange. Acceptance, recognition, and respect have all been shared between you in the spirit of Integrity. Thus you have quickly taken a major step toward resolving your difficulties and restoring harmony to this relationship. (By the way, I wonder if you noticed the "measuring" principle at work in this example.)

Again let's recognize that it is usually by much practice, patience, and forgiveness that partners in marriage learn to accept and acknowledge one another instead of judging right and wrong. But as they do so, *they establish an atmosphere of mutual respect in which each one can talk honestly about his (her) own experience and truly be heard by the other.* Beliefs, thoughts, feelings, desires, preferences, and reactions, including even the lingering tendency to judge one another, can be discussed openly and productively when *the primary purpose of the communication is to come to greater harmony through mutual understanding, which allows conflicts to be resolved in complete fairness to all concerned.*

At first, however, it is not uncommon to find yourself talking about your feelings and reactions in a subtle and often unconscious attempt to pass judgment, induce feelings of guilt, or otherwise control your partner's behavior. For example, what might be your purpose in saying to him (her), "Oh, I felt so *bad* when you said that to me last night!"? Are you saying this to release some emotional energy? To control your partner's behavior by trying to make him (her) feel guilty? To "get even" by making him (her) suffer for "hurting" you?

Of course there are times when all of us feel the need to "let off some steam" after an unpleasant experience. But as long as you allow judgment and manipulation to stand in the way of unconditional acceptance, you will find your days of harmony vanishing in the wake of growing conflict.

"But what if I really *did* feel bad?"

Then say so! But check your purpose. Your self-disclosure will contribute much to your marriage when you have outgrown your tendency to judge, and *your primary purpose is to come to greater harmony through mutual understanding, which allows conflicts to be resolved in complete fairness to all concerned.*

Communication in sex

Perhaps there is no more sensitive indicator of the kind of communication that prevails between husband and wife than the state of their sexual relationship. In fact, sex is itself a most powerful form of communication. Aside from its function in childbearing, it can reflect their acceptance and acknowledgment of one another, and so become a beautiful instrument for giving, and for sharing their most sublime feelings of appreciation for one another. But it can also be reduced to a dry and empty exercise in self-gratification, or to nothing at all. Or it can (and so often does) become the most destructive weapon of manipulation in the relationship.

However, when Integrity, mutual commitment, trust, unconditional acceptance,

and acknowledgment are established between a man and a woman in marriage,
their communication will express a growing desire to *give—to share the best that
is in them with one another . . . and with
the world. And nowhere will this gracious
spirit be more clearly reflected than in the
sexual relationship of that man and
woman.*

This, dear reader, is *productive* communication. *This* is the process in marriage that
produces lasting harmony, intimacy, and
fulfillment—the fondest ideals in the heart
of every sincere person who says, "I will."

Chapter Seven

Intimacy

We need only listen to ourselves talk about our hopes and dreams to recognize the value we place upon that warm and very personal (and not necessarily sexual) closeness we call *intimacy*. It's no secret that many couples decide to marry largely because they have enjoyed a measure of intimacy and want "to have and to hold" it for life. Indeed, their greatest hope is to share *a steadily growing and deepening experience of close friendship, affection, and sexual fulfillment.*

So they take the big step, and many of them wind up losing most of what they started with before the end of the first year! Then they blame one another for being unwilling or unable to do what is necessary to get it back. They think about starting over with someone new. And some just give up and "settle down" into lives of quiet mediocrity. All because they don't realize what is required to support *a steadily growing and deepening experience of close friendship, affection, and sexual fulfillment* in marriage. In terms of the pyramid we have been building in this book, these couples have tried to establish this intimacy on "thin air" instead of first putting a solid foundation under it!

The structure of the marriage pyramid

Look again at the diagram on page 89. Notice that every element of the marriage relationship we have considered in the foregoing chapters of this book follows from something more basic than itself: *Integrity* is the character of Life and Its universe; *mutual commitment*—the *identity* of the marriage relationship—is an expression of the partners' Integrity; *trust* is established on the basis of mutual commitment; *unconditional acceptance* is founded upon trust; *acknowledgment* is the expression of unconditional acceptance; *productive communication* begins with acknowledgment; and *intimacy* is the natural outcome of productive communication.

From productive communication to intimacy

How many times have we heard other people (if not ourselves) say, "Oh, how we used to be able to *talk* to each other before we got married!" Yes, they were so warmly interested in knowing more about one another, that each listened closely and really tried to understand the other's point of view. Their mutual attraction together with their respective dreams of finding the ideal partner left them eager to believe the best about each other. And in that wonderfully positive atmosphere, each one often felt inspired to treat the other with the same care and consideration as he himself or she herself would want to be treated. So naturally they felt a wonderful intimacy growing between them.

Now does the *order* of what is described here seem a bit familiar to you? Well, it should, because this typical scenario beautifully illustrates the operation of the "measuring" principle and the Golden Rule, which we have discussed at length in this book. Notice especially that what moved these people toward intimacy was their predisposition to believe the best about one another. However, it must be obvious to you by now that something more substantial than mutual attraction and hope is required for one to *continue* to believe the best about one's partner after the "honeymoon" is over. And that substantial *something* is the solid structure pictured by our marriage pyramid.

As stated in the previous chapter, *the primary purpose of productive communication is to come to greater harmony through mutual understanding, which allows conflicts to be resolved in complete fairness to all concerned.* In other words, "productive" communication *produces* mutual understanding; mutual understanding *produces* harmony; and the harmony of mutual understanding is the heart and soul of intimacy. It is also a fact that nothing so strengthens and deepens marital intimacy as does the process of resolving conflicts through mutual understanding. Why? Because *it provides the greatest opportunity for both partners to give the very best of themselves in one another's behalf, and be acknowledged for it!* And how wonderfully this works to sustain and increase their predisposition to believe the best about each other!

In such a climate as this, affection flows more and more freely between the partners, and their sexual communication becomes increasingly spontaneous and creative, inspired by ever-deepening mutual feelings of appreciation, admiration, and respect. This is human intimacy in its fullest dimension, and it brings with it an unique sense of fulfillment that can only be found in a genuine marriage.

Whether we are inclined toward marriage or not, all of us long for relationships in which a true spirit of friendship prevails. We want very deeply to establish closeness with others whom we can admire and trust, because we know intuitively that it is in the company of such people, who likewise trust and admire us, that we are inspired to *dis-cover* and to *live* the very best that is within us—to express our Integrity. This is the special kind of freedom that a true marriage can bestow upon its faithful partners. And what a wondrous paradox it is that their "binding" mutual commitment can lead to their greatest liberation!

Chapter Eight

The Nature
of Life

In your reading up to this point, I wonder if you have felt something was missing from these pages. Have you noticed that *love* is not mentioned *anywhere* in the preceding seven chapters of this book? Has this disturbed you?

Of course, this omission has been intentional.

It is often said that words are cheap, and you and I *know* that, in this category, the word *love* is at the very top of the list! The fact is, we each have our own images and concepts of love which we declare and often stubbornly defend, yet how very few of us really have any clear idea of what we're talking about!

However, in getting to the final chapter in your reading of this book, you have evidenced a strong desire to replace all those cheap words with your own certain experience of *knowing* what marriage is and exactly how it works.

So when we speak of "love" in marriage, what do we mean specifically? A collection of warm feelings, perhaps? Sexual attraction and involvement? Deeply caring about one's partner? Caring for one's partner's "needs"? Or does *love* include all of these?

What Love *is*

I speak from my own experience as I tell you that what you are about to read will be sufficient to transform the character of all your relationships for the rest of your life, if you will just study and ponder it in the depths of your heart until you experience the truth of it for yourself. What you have before you right now is a golden moment of opportunity. And you are either ready to accept its challenge and its reward, or you are not. It is that simple. . . .

Now what is *Love* with a capital "L"?

As with all things, you can begin to answer this question by looking at your own experience. First of all, you know that you have a basic *Love* for Life. That is, *you recognize, appreciate, and respect the value of the Life you are,* and, being of sound mind, you want to keep on living, even when things aren't going well for you. Under ideal conditions, of course, you often find yourself positively rejoicing in your own aliveness, don't you? In fact, this fundamental Love for Life is so strong that you may even be willing to risk your human life in some kind of dangerous sport or adventure just for the excitement value of the challenge—the chance to feel a greater sense of being alive!

Now who and what is this *you* who is experiencing all this Love for Life? *Individual Life* is who and what *you* are. Therefore, you can see from your own experience of loving the Life you are, that, fundamentally, *Love is Life recognizing, appreciating, respecting, and rejoicing in Itself.* And because you have experienced this Love, you already *know* It directly in your heart without first having to think about It or read about It in this book! Your reading has simply allowed you to "*re*-cognize" It, which means to *again* (re) be aware of (cognize) It within yourself.

Love is Life recognizing, appreciating, respecting, and rejoicing in Itself. It is just as natural to Life as Integrity (order and completeness) is, and we have already established that you cannot not have

Integrity. Now it remains for you to *recognize* the fact that *you cannot not have Love!* Just as *Integrity* is always present as the character of Life whether you are acting according to It or not, so *Love* is always present as the nature of Life, whether you are feeling and expressing It or not.

YOU CANNOT NOT HAVE LOVE. Your strong desire to survive stands as sufficient proof of this by itself, doesn't it? Moreover, you can trace every single desire you are capable of having right back to the one most fundamental desire you have in common with all of humankind, which is *the desire to express and experience Love.* Even your basic desire for survival has *this* desire behind it!

High achievement, wealth, fame, pleasure, power—the desire for any or all of these has its basis in the desire to express and experience more Love, hence enjoy a greater sense of Life. Men and women of great accomplishment so often say, "I *love* my work so much. I just couldn't imagine doing anything else!" Those who seek wealth, fame, and power usually do so with the intention of sharing themselves with others in some way and being loved for it. Frequently, a great deal of selfish human ego, excess, and abuse may be involved, but the "prime mover" underneath all of these distorted desires and practices is the basic desire to express and experience Love—*Life's recognizing, appreciating, respecting, and rejoicing in Its own Integrity and value.*

Love is the very nature of the Life we are. Yet if we are unaware that we already have an abundance of Love within ourselves, we try to get It from the outside world, sometimes to the point of becoming highly self-centered and obsessed with seeking wealth, fame, pleasure, and power.

Of course, a significant part of our most basic desire is to experience the Love of others, especially That of our partners in marriage. But how can we ever hope to do so as long as we believe we don't have enough Love within ourselves and therefore *need* to *get* It from someone else? On what basis are you going to trust that your partner has Love enough to keep giving It to you, if you believe *you* don't have enough even for yourself, and therefore need his or her Love to make you complete?

Are you beginning to see something here?

Again and again throughout this book it has been pointed out that the "measuring" principle governs our daily experience of life. It says, "With what measure you measure, it will be measured to you." Therefore, *what is being measured to you must always be what you have been measuring.* This is the

Integrity (order) of Life operating in our human affairs. Now, in the light of this principle and the Golden Rule ("Always treat others as you would like them to treat you"), can you see any way to *get* the experience of another person's Love with any consistency at all except as a reflection ("measured to you") of the Love *you* are "measuring"? *Of course not!*

But please remember that the principle means *you determine the quality of your own experience, regardless of what others may do.* Therefore, even though your parents or others close to you might be consistently expressing Love to you, you will not be able to understand and appreciate It as genuine Love until you first become aware of the fact that you already have Love within yourself, and then begin to express It.

Now can you see why the wisdom of "Love your neighbor *as yourself*" is still with us after so many centuries?

Take some time now to ponder the
following questions carefully: How could
you know Love, Integrity, Beauty, Harmony,
or anything else of value in Life if It were
not already within you? On what other basis
could you possibly *re-*cognize It? How
could you appreciate the Beauty of a sunset
if Beauty were not already alive within you
as the standard for *re-*cognizing what is
beautiful? And how could those around you
be aware of the same Beauty if It were not
within them, too? How could you *re-*cognize
anything you have read about Love, Integrity,
and Principle if These were not already
within the Life *you* are? And if you are aware
that you already have Love, can you still
feel the *need* to *get* It from somebody else
in order to complete yourself?

It is a simple fact that *you cannot feel
Love and need at the same time.* As long
as your attention is occupied with a sense
of *need*, it is impossible for you to feel

genuine *Love*, much less express It to another. However, when you are truly *recognizing, appreciating, respecting, and rejoicing in the Integrity and value of the Life YOU are*, you do not any longer feel the need to *get* this Love from others. Instead you begin to *recognize, appreciate, respect, and rejoice in the Integrity and value of the Life of the people around you.* You come to experience a deep sense of togetherness (unity, *one*ness) with those closest to you, and the deeper meaning of "Love your neighbor *as yourself*" becomes clear to you. The Truth of Love has opened your heart and made you free of need. Now you are inspired to express It in ever more beautiful ways! And this you can do with no thought of "getting," because the "measuring" principle ensures that the same shall be returned to you.

Of course, there are those times, particularly in marriage, when you may forget the Love within you and again feel that old sense of need. But you will have the support of your partner's Love in these moments, and they will occur less and less frequently as your inner experience of genuine Love increases.

Love is the substance and the fulfillment of marriage. Love is spontaneous and free. It does not operate in response to a demand. Love gives for the joy of sharing. It begs for nothing in return.

"Love possesses not nor would it be possessed; for Love is sufficient unto Love. . . . Love has no other desire but to fulfill Itself" (Gibran).

What Love *does* in marriage

Perhaps you have already guessed that Love is the real subject of the first seven chapters of this book. What you have read there is actually a description of what Love *does* in marriage. Therefore, it can be said that *the marriage pyramid is a picture of the expression of Love:*

Of course, this pyramid does not signify an actual division of the marriage relationship into separated levels, however it might appear to the casual reader. Rather, it represents marriage as *one indivisible whole,* a system of order, and the "levels" are meant to show how the various processes are interrelated, and how they follow, one from another, to make up *the whole,* which *is* the expression of Love in the form we call marriage.

A final word

Dear reader, what you have just read has a depth of meaning and value that can dramatically change the course of your life. But it cannot be fully realized in a single reading. Therefore, I ask that you study this final chapter until its meaning is clear to you. Then go back to the Introduction and read the whole book again, remembering that the first seven chapters represent the progressive unfoldment of the expression of Love.

Study this book as a presentation of what

Love *is* and what Love *does* in marriage. Keep it as your close companion. Share it with your partner or partner-to-be. Read and contemplate this message each day until your heart gives you your own realization of the truth that is written here. Then find someone who needs *The Secret of Staying Together* . . . and give it away.